The Self-Taught Developer

Tommy Chheng

Contents

Chapter 1

Introduction

> "We are stuck with technology when what we really want is just stuff that works."
>
> — Douglas Adams, The Salmon of Doubt

Everywhere you look you'll see software involved. From the mobile apps on your iPhone to financial banking machines to science fields like biology. The idea of the self-taught developer is becoming commonplace out of necessity. Having programming skills will inevitably help you in your future career even if your goal is not to become a full-time developer.

This book will not be your only source for learning to program. Throughout this book, I will reference many other sources which I encourage you to explore.

I wrote this book to supplement the self-taught developer with useful information from work experience as well as the practical bits of computer science classes in a traditional university.

Who is this book for?

You could be:

- The biologist who needs to learn enough programming to analyze your data.
- The MBA graduate who has a startup idea.
- The career switcher who wants a programming job.
- The college student struggling with the dry university computer science classes.

This book just assumes you have a desire to learn programming and perhaps you have already started learning.

On a minor note, I will be using the terms programmer, developer and software engineer interchangeably. There are some subtle differences around these terms but for the purposes of this book, assume they are the same.

How can I use this book?

I recommend you skim through the book once and use it as a reference when you run into each issue.

Throughout this book, I will use different programming languages as examples. If a code example looks unfamiliar to you, look up the programming language documentation on the Internet to help you read and understand it. Regardless of the language, most of the syntax and concepts will be similar.

The objective of this book isn't to learn a particular language, it is to make you a better **self-taught developer**.

Chapter 2

How to Start

Prepare to Invest Your Time

You won't learn programming in a day. If you want to become a skillful developer, prepare to invest many hours in mindful practice.

Focus by Setting Goals

I recommend you start your programming journey with expectations. Don't say "I want to learn to program in 6 months." It is more useful to learn with specific goals. Set concrete measurable goals for yourself:

- "I want to build a 2D flappy bird game for the iPhone"
- "I want to build a web app that lets people share calendars"
- "I want to build a robot to move a camera"

With a goal, you can start creating a plan and the topics you need to learn.

Programming is never-ending: you will always have to learn something new. You might have to learn a new language, a new tool, or how to use a new library.

If you were interested in frontend programming in 2010, you might have learned jQuery or Backbone JS. In 2020, you would be learning React or Vue.js.

If you were interested in data science between 2010 and 2020, you might have started learning Python and then had to discover how to use iPython or Jupyter Notebooks in your workflow.

By choosing a goal and having a learning mindset, you can set your learning path accordingly for more efficient learning.

Expect to be Frustrated

You will get frustrated during your journey. Even programmers with 10 years of experience will hit problems they have to spend a large amount of time to fix. But know that most problems you encounter are solvable and have probably been solved by someone else.

A Typical Approach to Learning

Every programmer, beginner or advanced can start learning by finding a guide to accomplish your goal like "how to use R to create a graph" or "creating a todo list app in Nodejs". This can be a blog post, Youtube video or published book.

You will then run into a problem which the guide doesn't cover. It is very rare that a guide will solve exactly what you want because programmers have different environment setups or data differences.

At this point, you can solve the problem with the experience of encountering a similar problem or concept.

Alternatively, you could search for the solution on Stackoverflow. As you become more experienced, you will learn different search queries to narrow down the search to find the right solution and realize if the results can be applied to your problem.

If you are completely unfamiliar with what you are doing, you will need to start with more focused learning on the topic.

Learn to Use a Computer

To be a decent programmer, you'll also need to know how to use a computer effectively. This means knowing how your computer generally works. This becomes more important when you need to debug why something isn't working.

Can you answer these quickly?

- What are files and directories? Which directories are on the root directory?
- How can you check how much disk space is left on your hard drive?
- Why is your computer being slow and how can you check why?

When I interview candidates, there are easy to spot habits which can help establish yourself as a skillful computer user:

- How do they navigate through directories on the command line?
- Can they use their code editor's many features?
- Can they perform computer tasks quickly like switching between different applications?
- Do they know where to look for help on the Internet if they are stuck?

Chapter 3

Sources to Learn From

The world isn't a test where you can't look online or through books for answers. Every resource is fair game to learn from.

Use multiple sources to learn a particular subject, rather than just one. You'll get different perspectives and see the commonalities/differences.

Pick a learning method that's most suited for you. If you do not have much self-motivation, maybe a dev bootcamp or a university extension course could be the forcing function. If you are self-motivated, online courses, podcasts and books will make it more flexible for you to learn on your own schedule.

Online Courses

Online courses are the best place to start your learning process. The structured plan helps new programmers stay focused on learning a topic at time.

- coursera.org offers more traditional programming education similar to university courses.
- freecodecamp.org offers a more hands-on experience to learn programming topics.

Web Communities

Below is a list of useful communities to visit on a frequent basis for help and advice.

- The Coding Den Discord Server The Coding Den is composed of multiple chat channels for you to ask programming questions and advice.

- dev.to Dev.to is a community where you can read daily articles written by programmers.

- reddit.com/r/learnprogramming A large Reddit community of over 1 million for general programming questions.

- reddit.com/r/cscareerquestions Get career advice on Reddit.

Conferences

Conferences can be expensive but many of them come with financial assistance. They are also useful for meeting people in the industry who may lead to a possible job down the road. I recommend attending conferences once you have some knowledge on the topic of the conference for it to be worthwhile. For example, if you want to attend RailsConf, learn and deploy a Rails application before attending.

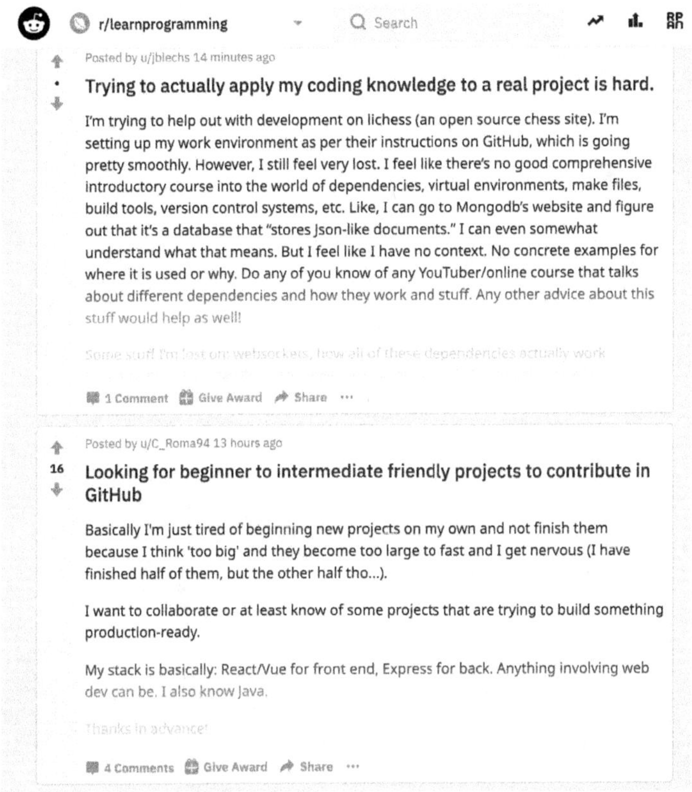

Figure 3.1: Reddit

Figure 3.2: The Coding Den Discord

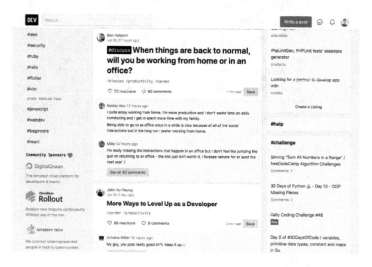

Figure 3.3: Dev.to Communtity

Developer Bootcamps

Developer bootcamps are varied in scope. Some are a month long, some are 8 hours a day lasting 6 months. The cost can vary as well, a dev boot camp can cost more than $10,000. A few have unique payment options including Lambda School and Flatiron School. Lambda School is free upfront but requires you to pay back with a percentage of your salary after you get a job. For Flatiron School, you can get your money back if you cannot get a job within 6 months.

Bootcamps help with the last mile of your learning process. Online courses will keep you limited to particular topics. The developer bootcamps will allow you access to an instructor and allow you to learn beyond the constraints of a topic in an online course.

To make the most effective use of your time, I recommend you start learning programming before starting a dev boot camp. This will allow you to ask dev bootcamp instructors deeper questions to speed up your learning process.

Videos

You can find video tutorials and explanations on Youtube. These videos can be topic-specific so you need to know what to look for. TechPrimers on Youtube is an example of a quality source. Additionally, you can watch a programmer write code on Youtube or Twitch.tv. I found this particularly useful for new programmers as it shows their thought process as they narrate how they solve something. A list of developer streams can be found at https://github.com/bnb/awesome-developer-streams

Podcasts

Podcasts serve as a great supplementary source of knowledge. They can introduce you to new topics and ideas. If you have the time, Subscribe to both general podcasts and technology specific ones.

Below are a few useful examples:

- Labybug Podcasts **A** podcast for all developers which discusses technology and careers.

- Software Engineering Daily **A** podcast that goes into great detail about a particular topic with a guest expert.

- Soft Skills Engineering **A** podcast that focuses about the workplace: pay raises, getting promoted, quitting your job, etc.

- The Bike Shed **A** podcast that primarily discusses Ruby on Rails and Javascript.

Books

Books are also great supplementary resources. There are some general timeless classics like Andrew Hunt's The Pragmatic Programmer or Martin Fowler's Refactoring.

There are also technology-dependent books like The Rails 6 Way that focuses on how a particular technology works. These books will become out-dated as the newer technology appears.

I observe newer programmers finding these technology-dependent books more useful since you can follow along with the exercises. Once you have a more solid foundation, the more general classics become more useful.

For some new programmers, they can read and read but never really learn anything. Actual programming time is far more important. Think of books as supplementary knowledge to level you up rather than the only source.

Community College and University Classes

You can take classes through a local community college or an extension program at a university. This gives you the benefit of taking a rigorous class without dedicating a complete 4 or 5 years to being enrolled. The additional benefit is meeting other students in a similar learning stage as you.

Mentors

This will be difficult because you need a mentor who has walked the path you want to take.

You also have to make it valuable for the mentor to contribute their own time. This means work on your part. Be prepared to enter meetings with expected topics: what you have learned, a problem you need help with possible solutions, etc.

Local meetups, co-workers, online web communities(Codingcoach.io) can be good sources to find a mentor.

Chapter 4

The Tools to Use

Code Editor

The first thing you need is to use a real code editor.

Code files are just text files, but when you see a real programmer, they are not using Microsoft Word. Use an editor suited for efficient coding tasks: typing fast, finding words, opening other files without using the mouse or trackpad.

I recommend Visual Studio Code if you are just getting started and don't know the command line too well. It is customizable for any programming language you may want to use.

Juypter Notebooks

If you are writing code to output a report like an A/B testing result or data analysis, consider using an interactive and share-able computing editor like Juypter Notebooks. This will allow you to share your code with others to run easily.

Figure 4.1: VS Code

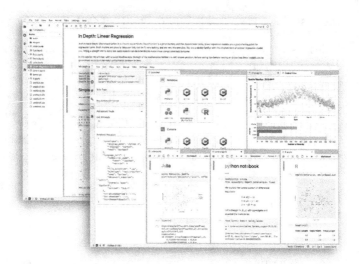

Figure 4.2: Jupyter Notebooks

Source Control

Source control is an absolute must for any coding project. Without it, co-workers would be sending files over email or Dropbox. Either of these are inferior to using a source control system.

Source control is the act of keeping track of the edits in your files. This allows you to go back to a previous version if a change you made broke the program. If multiple people are working on the same project, source control is vital to avoid project members overwriting each other's work.

Git

`git` is the most used source control system. There are others like Subversion and Mercurial but just stick with learning `git` because it is the most prevalent tool in the community.

The bare minimum of amount of learning `git` commands are:

```
git init
git add .
git commit -m "Write a description about your changes"
git push
```

Here's a free book you can read online for how to use `git` effectively:
git-scm.com/book/en/v2

When you use `git` in a team of one, it's fairly easy and it's an effective backup tool and allows you to use the project on multiple projects.

Once you use `git` in a team of more than one, it becomes much more complex in management because of possible conflicts. However, it's also much better than the alternative of copying and pasting code from your team members.

I recommend GitHub or GitLab as a free git hosting source to store your projects.

The Command Line

The command line is a way of working with a computer where you type in commands as opposed to pointing and clicking buttons.

On a Mac, you can launch the app, `Terminal` to get to the command line.

You will commonly see the command line referenced as the `Terminal`, `Console` or `Shell`. At the beginner level, you can think of them as the same.

UNIX and Linux System Administration Handbook is a comprehensive guide for getting proficient at the command line.

Common Command Line Programs

Here are the most common command line programs you will be using:

- `ls` - list the contents of the current directory
- `cd` - navigate to a directory
- `pwd` - list the current working directory
- `mkdir` - create a directory
- `grep` - find a particular text in a list of files
- `cat` - show the contents of a file
- `head` - show the first few lines of a file
- `tail` - show the last few lines of a file
- `ps` - show which programs are running
- `top` - show the current usage of the CPU and memory
- `kill` - quit a particular program
- `ssh` - log into another machine
- `scp` - copy a file to another machine
- `curl` - print the contents of a web link

Is there a command line program used that you don't understand? You can type in `man [command]` and it will show you the documentation for it.

Windows has a different set of command line tools. If you have a Windows machine, you can enable Windows Subsystem for Linux and then install the Ubuntu Linux system. This will let you use these common set of command line programs.

Example Command Line

Here's an example command you can input:

```
> ls -al tempo
```

`ls` is the program and `-al` and `tempo` are known as the arguments.

Typing in `man ls` will explain how to use the `ls` command:

```
NAME
     ls -- list directory contents

SYNOPSIS
     ls [-ABCFGHLOPRSTUW@abcdefghiklmnopqrstuwx1%] [file]

DESCRIPTION
     For each operand that names a file of a type
     other than directory,
     ls displays its name as well as any requested,
     associated information.
     For each operand that names a file of type directory,
     ls displays the names of files contained
     within that directory..
```

This Stack Exchange question goes over the details of the command line parts in more detail: https://unix.stackexchange. com/q/416945

Longer Example

Here's an example session of a series of commands that you run
together:

- copying a file on your laptop to another machine
- logging into that machine
- seeing the first few lines of the file
- compiling the project
- running a program with that file as an input
- logging out of that machine
- copying the output back to your machine

```
scp input.fasta ec2-user@aws.com:~
ssh ec2-user@aws.com
head input.fasta
make all
./program input.fasta > output.csv
exit
scp ec2-user@aws.com:~/output.csv .
```

Chapter 5

Running Code

As a programmer, you may not have to write a single line of code to accomplish a task.

Often, you can find existing code that does nearly what you need. Even if you do not know the programming language that the code is written in, that does not prevent you from using the code.

If you are lucky, the author will have written a README file describing exactly what you need to do to run it. Be warned that this is not the case most often. Most software you find will have half-working instructions and you will have to find help on how to run the project.

Build Systems

Typically a programmer will use a standard build system to "build" the project.

For most C/C++ programs, there is generally a `Makefile` in the root of the program directory. You can usually just type `make all` to compile the program into an executable which you can run.

Other build systems you may encounter are:

- Java: `maven`, `gradle`
- Node.js: `npm`
- Ruby: `rake`

Streams and Pipes

`Stdin`, `stdout`, `stderr` is a fundamental concept of the terminal/command line environment and useful when running programs. These streams let your program interact with you and other programs.

- Stdin (standard input) - data going into a program
- Stdout (standard output) - data going out of a program
- Stderr (standard error output) - error data going out of a program

Typically, stdin is a stream going from a keyboard to a program. Instead of a keyboard, the input can come from a file as well.

Likewise, stdout is a stream going from a program to the terminal screen. Instead of a terminal screen, you can also have the output go straight to a file.

For example:

```
ls -l > output.txt
```

This is saying run the `ls` program and redirect the stdout output to the `output.txt` file. You can open the file and see it's the same output as if you ran the command and saw the output on the terminal screen.

Instead of just redirecting **stdout**, you can also send a program's **stdout** output to another program's **stdin** input using pipes.

The concept of pipes is one of the fundamental designs of Unix. Pipes allow you to easily chain a group of commands together where the output of one program becomes the input of the next.

For example, there is a unix command called `history` which lists the last few commands you previously executed. `grep` lets you find lines from `stdin` matching a string or pattern.

If you run `history | grep home`, you are asking the operating system to run `history` first and send its output to `grep` so this command will find your previously typed commands which included the word `home`

Running Programs in the Background

Sometimes you will have a program that takes hours to run on the server. When you log off(willing or unexpected) the server, the program will also quit.

Of course you don't want to be at the computer screen all day while it runs.

You can run a program in the background with the **bg** command but an easier way is to use `screen`.

Screen lets you run the program in a session. When you log back into the machine, you can resume the session again.

For example, you have a program `run.sh` that you want to run over night on a server.

- Log into the server using `ssh`.
- Start screen by typing in `screen`
- Start your program ie. `./run.sh`
- Now you can just close the terminal program
- [5 hours later]
- SSH back into the server.
- Resume your session with `screen -r`

Shell Scripting

When you want to automate running a list of programs with the output of one program being fed into another program, you will want to use shell scripts.

Shell scripting languages like `zsh` or `bash` are useful for quick ways you can use to write a pipeline of programs together.

Interpreted vs Compiled Languages

Compiled languages(C, C++) require more steps for writing code than interpreted languages. Compiled languages require the programmer to:

- write code
- run a compiler to translate the code into machine-readable code
- run the machine-readable code

Interpreted languages(R, Python, Ruby) skip the compiler stage:

- write code
- run the code through the language's runtime/virtual machine that translates into machine code on the fly

Code translation using virtual machines tends to have slower performance. Note that the term virtual machine should not be confused with operating system virtualization software like VirtualBox. Virtual machines are a similar concept but it's used in the context of just code translation like running a Java program on your Mac whereas Virtualbox is used in the context of running whole operating systems inside another like running a test Windows VM on your Mac.

There are hybrid languages like Java/C# that feature virtual machines running partially compiled code rather than the raw source code.

Hybrid compiled/interpreted languages require programmers to:

- write code
- run a compiler to translate the code to a partially compiled code
- run the compiled code through the virtual machine, translating it to machine-readable code

Using a Different Language

This is a very important concept: Just because you do not know everything about another programming language, it does not stop you from using a program written in that language.

Learn the basics of how to run the program and you interact with the program through its interface which could be files or through a web server.

Here are three examples of how to run a simple program that prints out "Hello World" written in different languages: C, Java, Python.

Add the code below to a file named hello.c:

```
#include <stdio.h>

int main(int argc, char **argv) {
    puts("Hello World\n");
    return 0;
}
```

Run this on the command line to compile the code:

```
gcc -o hello hello.c
./hello
```

Add the code below to a file named `hello.java`:

```
public class Hello {
    public static void main(String[] args) {
        System.out.println("Hello World");
    }
}
```

Run this on the command line:

```
javac Hello.java
java Hello
```

Add the code below to a file named `hello.py`:

```
print("Hello World\n");
```

Run this on the command line:

```
python hello.py
```

Running your Program in the Cloud

You can run code on your laptop. But your laptop could be dog slow. You will need to learn to run your program on another machine.

What do people mean when they are running their applications in the cloud?

The cloud refers to a seemingly unlimited group of computers you can rent from. The most common and accessible vendor is Amazon AWS. Microsoft Azure and Google Cloud Platform are competitors you can also use.

Once you create an Amazon AWS account, you can rent a machine by the hour. This can be as cheap as 0.05 an hour. The faster and the more memory, the more expensive it is.

You will need to use `ssh` to log into the machine and `scp` to move files between your computer to the remote machine you rented.

Chapter 6

Reading Code

> "Less than 10% of the code has to do with the ostensible purpose of the system; the rest deals with input-output, data validation, data structure maintenance, and other housekeeping."

— Mary Shaw

Reading code is difficult because it does not convey the programmer's intentions. It includes all of the little workarounds and attempts at trying to get the program to work.

You will need to learn to read code as a skill.

When you join a project, the first thing you will have to do is get up to speed with the current set of code that has been written.

The Starting Points in a Project

Start with the README file in the main directory. This should guide you on the structure of the code project.

If you are lucky, the project has tests which show you direct examples on how to use code.

Entry Point

A program always has an entry point. Sometimes a program may have multiple entry points like a command line program and a web server component. Finding these entry points is really helpful to start reading a code base. For command line scripts, it is just the script itself. Other programs might have a `main` function.

Documentation

Usually there is a function being used but you don't know what it does. Each language tends to have its own documentation available.

Consider the data structure, `set`. For Python, you can just type in `pydoc set` on the command line and see what it does and what methods are available for it.

Likewise, Ruby has `rdoc` for its command line documentation lookup tool.

Following that, Google is your next option.

Conventional Project Directory Structure

Does the project follow a conventional project directory structure? Knowing which files are in which directories will help your knowledge of the project.

For example, in a Ruby on Rails project, it is a common convention to separate code files into known directories like `controllers`, `models`, and `views`. A programmer proficient in Ruby on Rails would know immediately where to look in these conventional directory names to make a necessary change.

Do your best to follow these conventions. You can search Google with [blank] `project directory structure` where [blank] can be a framework(ie. Ruby on Rails, Django, Express) or language(ie. Java, Python) to learn more.

Code Reading Tips

Understand how variables change

Reading code is often more difficult when a program has a lot of variables that change.

This is most apparent in a `for` loop.

One way to understand how a variable changes is to create a table with all the variables as they change across time steps.

Here is an example of x variable changing inside a `for` loop during each step:

```
length = 3;
x = 1;
for (i = 0; i < length; i++) {
    x += i;
}
```

$i = 0$ $x = 1$
$i = 1$ $x = 2$
$i = 2$ $x = 3$

Here is a more complex example with a `for` loop inside a `for` loop:

```
length = 3;
x = 1;
y = 2;
for (i = 0; i < length; i++) {
    x += i;
```

```
    for (j = 0; j < length; j++) {
        y += i + j;
    }
}
```

$i = 0$ x $= 1$
$i = 0$ x $= 1$, y $= 1$
$i = 0$ x $= 1$, y $= 2$
...

Ideally, you want to avoid writing code that involves a lot of variables changing, but code like this exists in the world.

Functions

When you read code, learn to trace code from the start to the end. This involves knowing where the entry point is and which functions are being called.

Language Skill Transfer

So you are most likely learning one language first. In reality, you will have to learn to read multiple languages.

Most languages have the basics:

- `int/float/string/arrays` data types
- `if` statements, `for/while` loops

Sometimes languages have the same thing but have different names:

- Ruby has a method named `select` which selects items from an array.

```
['astro', 'cap'].select{|item| item == 'astro'}
```

returns `['astro']`

javascript has a method named`filter` which does the same thing:

```
['astro', 'cap'].filter(item => item === 'astro')
```

returns `['astro']`

I find it helpful to be really proficient in one language when you are starting to learn. In contrast, if you try to be an expert in multiple languages, you won't have the time to learn enough depth of one to be useful. After learning one language, you can translate what you know into a different set of syntax.

Chapter 7

Writing Understandable Code

"plans are worthless but planning is everything"

— Dwight Eisenhower

The idea of following a plan to the tee is unlikely but the process of planning involves thinking through the options is invaluable in guiding what you will be doing.

To write understandable code, the work begins even before writing the first line of code.

A major point of wanting to write understandable code is that it reduces the possibilities of bugs. Bugs can happen when you can't easily reason what the code is doing and you are guessing to see what the code will do.

When you write code, you aren't writing it just to work, you are writing it for someone else to understand it (even if it's your future self).

Write a README

The first step towards understandable code is not the code itself but the project description. Each project should have a README file as a summary of the project and how to use it.

The HTML/CSS framework project, Bootstrap has a good example of a README file

```
Quick start

Four quick start options are available:

Download the latest release.

Clone the repo:
    git clone https://github.com/twbs/bootstrap.git
Install with npm:
    npm install bootstrap.

Read the Getting started page for information on the
framework contents, templates and examples, and more.
```

This README file answers the following questions:

- What is the project used for?
- How can a developer install the project?
- What software dependencies are needed to install it?
- How did you organize the files in the project?

Learn about the Domain

What is the purpose of the program you are writing for? Is it for a banking company? Real estate? It is useful to learn about the domain you are involved in. The knowledge will be useful when you are creating the classes, functions and variable names as well as when you need to explain how your program works.

Learn to Diagram

You need to be able to think of your projects in diagrams. Diagrams help you plan out how to build your new project or understand an existing project. It is also a great visualization to inform your non-technical audiences. In the project you are working on, you should be able to draw out the objects used, the input/output data flow and the interactions between the software and the user.

During interviews, these diagrams are known as the dreaded whiteboard systems problems where you are at a blank whiteboard and you are asked to diagram a particular system.

Below are a few different types of diagrams used to describe software projects.

Sequence Diagram

I find sequence diagrams the most important to learn. A sequence diagram shows how different objects interact across time.

You can use sequence diagrams to understand a series of function calls or network requests between servers.

Class Diagram

Class diagrams are most useful for showing the relationships of objects in your program or system to yourself and even non-programmers.

These objects are often stored in database tables. There are different ways to represent objects and their relationships. Class diagrams help you and others understand your choice in designing the representation.

For example, if you were writing a web application for a physical trainer who wants to sell training plans. What do you name each object? Are you using terms like "trainers", "athletes" or

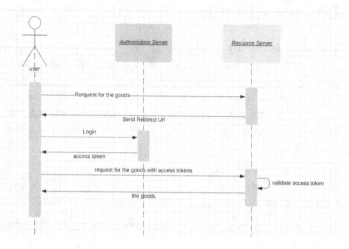

Figure 7.1: Sequence Diagram of Web Requests

more generic terms like "user"? Which attributes do you store with each object? Do you store workouts of a training plan in one database table or as separate tables?

A class diagram would answer these questions in a more clear manner than a paragraph of text or just the program code.

State Machine Diagram

State machine diagrams help you understand how state changes in your program.

I find state machine diagrams helpful in finding possible design issues with invalid transiting states.

One example is showing the workflow of paying for a subscription service.

A subscription state can be: pending, active, paused, non-renewed and cancelled

For example, it should not be possible for a trial pending state to transition directly into a non-renewed state. A state machine

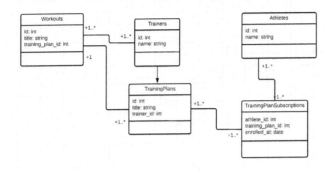

Figure 7.2: Class Diagram Example

diagram can show the possible and not possible transitions.

More Diagrams

See https://creately.com/blog/diagrams/uml-diagram-types-examples/ for more examples of other useful diagrams.

C4 Model

Another type of diagramming is the C4 Model. Simon Brown created the C4 model to help you diagram your project at different zoom levels. Think of it as the Google Maps for diagrams. Sometimes you want to see all the states in the country for the highways. Sometimes you need to zoom into a city to see all the local streets. Software diagrams work in a similar way.

Depending on how you want to analyze your project or present it, you want to diagram it on a different zoom level. C4 stands for the different zoom levels: context, containers, components, and code.

Check C4model.com for more information on this type of diagramming.

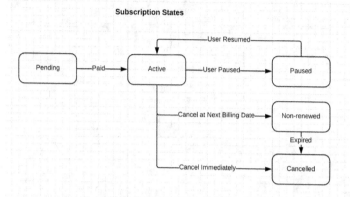

Figure 7.3: State Machine Diagram Example

Diagramming Tools

You can start with just a pen and paper to start practicing diagrams. Once you want to start with your diagrams, I recommend using an online tool like diagrams.net or Lucidchart. This will allow you to work with others and update the diagram as your project changes.

Use Dependency Management

When you first start coding, you may have copied and pasted code you found on the internet. Someone might have just emailed you a zip file containing a lot of code. You just unzipped these into your project directory to use.

While this may work, there are inherent problems.

What if the code had a bug?

Would you have to copy and paste the updated code into your code?

You'll want to use a dependency management system.

Each language has its own solution to dependency management. Ruby has `ruby gems`. Python has `pip packages`, Node has `npm modules`, Java has `jars`.

In dependency management systems, programmers package their projects into a package(also referred to as library or module).

Using these packaging systems will allow you to easily update to the latest changes and fixes.

Versioning

You probably have seen the software with the version number: ie. Ruby 2.1.1.

These version numbers let people know which software they need and which one works with another piece of software.

Typically version numbers follow the Semantic Versioning convention which has 3 parts: Major.Minor.Revision

The first number, the major number means that software written for different major numbers will not work together or that it has significant changes.

The last two numbers, the minor and revision numbers mean there was a set of bugfixes and software written with different minor versions will work together.

Follow the semantic versioning convention for any software you write if you need to label it with a version.

Write Functions

If you ever read a section of code that is greater than 100 lines, you probably found it hard to understand. Divide your code into functions. They make your code more understandable. They let you reuse the code elsewhere in your problem. They make things easier to change in the future. Instead of changing code in 5 places, you change it in one place.

When to Write Comments

Write comments for function headers and whenever the intent of the code needs to be clarified.

Avoid writing comments if reading the code is just as clear.

Here's an example of bad comments:

```
const schema = new Schema({
    id:   Schema.Types.ObjectId,
    // the user id
    userId: Schema.Types.ObjectId,
    // this is the title
    title: String,
});
```

These comments offer no new knowledge over the variable name itself.

Here's a better example of good comment:

```
const schema = new Schema({
    id:   Schema.Types.ObjectId,
    //the trainer id
    userId: Schema.Types.ObjectId,
    // This is the app name on the launcher screen.
    // Example: Climber Workouts
    title: String,
});
```

These comments tell you the context of how the variable will be used and gives an example.

Name Class/Function/Variable By Intent

Naming things is one of the more difficult processes in programming.

Any code you write will be read by someone, even if it's yourself 5 months from now.

There are different places where you need to consider naming things:

- filenames
- directory names
- module/package
- class names
- functions
- classes

Name things after their intent rather than what it is:

- use `destination` not `tmpString1`
- use `source` not `tmpString2`

Name Variable Names as positive, not negative

A variable named with a positive name like `isActive` is more understandable than `isInactive`

Imagine reading `if (isActive)` or `if (!isInactive)`. Both mean the same thing, but which is more understandable?

under_score vs camelCase

When you write variable and function names with multiple words, you usually have two choices on how to write these:

Underscores : `text_view` or `compute_function()` Camel case : `textView` or `computeFunction()`

Do not use both ways of naming variables in your project. Typically the programming language has a guideline which you should follow.

Code Spacing Matters

Can you spot the error in this code?

```
var compare = function(choice1, choice2) {
    if (choice1 === choice2) {
        return "tie!";
        }
      else if (choice1 === "scissors") {
            if (choice2 === "rock") {
            return "rock";
        }
        else {
            return "scissors";
        }
};
```

How about now?

```
var compare = function(choice1, choice2) {
    if (choice1 === choice2) {
        return "tie!";
    } else if (choice1 === "scissors") {
        if (choice2 === "rock") {
            return "rock";
        } else {
            return "scissors";
        }
};
```

All I did was line the spacing so they match up. You can
more easily see there is a missing } in the second example. Be
pedantic and consistent in spacing.

Linting

Lint checks your code for bugs and suggests how to format it
to make it easier to read.

Every language has a linting program. Python has `pep8`,
Javascript has `eslint`.

One step further is prettier.io. You can setup your editor to
run this tool on any of your files and instantly format it.

Use these to make your code look professionally formatted.

Statements vs Expressions

You can think of each line of code as a statement or an expression. A statement does not return back a value. Expressions
do return back a value. You can use expressions like (x > 5)
to shorten your code.

Don't do:

```
function isGreaterThanFive(x) {
    if (x > 5) {
        return true;
    } else {
        return false;
    }
}
```

You can just write:

```
function isGreaterThanFive(x) {
    return x > 5;
}
```

Coding Style

Find your language's coding style and follow it!

Sometimes different people have different opinions of coding style so just pick one set and follow it. These arguments can be endlessly pointless like using tabs vs spaces. I think it's just important to select one and be consistent.

Best Practices

Look up "best practices" for the language you are writing for. This is a good way to preemptively avoid the most common problems.

Here's an example of "Android best practices" https://github. com/futurice/android-best-practices#resources

Avoid Deep Nesting of if Statements

```
if () {
  if () {

  }
} else {

}
```

can be written as:

```
if (!) {
}
```

Separate Long if Expressions

If you have multiple expressions in your if statements, you can separate them into variables and reference them in the if statements. This can allow you to test each expression as well.

```
if ((x < 20 && x > 0) || (y < 5 && y > 0)) {
...
}
```

to:

```
is_x_valid = x < 20 && x > 0
is_y_valid = y < 5 && y > 0
if (is_x_valid && is_y_valid) {
...
}
```

Write Short Functions

A function should do one thing. Once a function starts doing more than one thing, break it up into smaller functions. The smaller each function is, the easier it is to test and verify its correctness.

Write Clear Code, not Clever Code

Clear code is understandable with a minimum amount of necessary knowledge. Clever code is an attempt to make something faster.

You can write code to divide a number by 2: x >> 1 or x / 2

The >> operator is a clever way of dividing by 2 because of the way the binary arithmetic works. Back in the old days, this could have been faster. Unless your program is largely dealing with binary, don't fall into these traps of being clever. Just write simple x / 2 which most people can understand.

Handling Errors

Even if you write the most correct code, the user of your program can still experience an error. For example, if your program reads from a file, that file can have an incorrect format or not even exist. If your program has code to handle the error, you can inform the user what the problem is.

There are two categories of error handling: returning error codes and throwing an exception. You'll see both styles.

Error Codes

One way of notifying the function caller of an error is to include it as part of the return value.

```
function getUser(email) {
  if (!email) {
    return {
      user: null,
      errorCode: NO_EMAIL_SPECIFIED,
      error: 'No email was specified.'
    };
  }
  const userJson = UserApi.findByEmail(email);
  if (!userJson) {
    return {
      user: null,
      errorCode: ITEM_NOT_FOUND,
      error: 'User not found'
    };
  }

  return {
    user: userJson,
    errorCode: null,
    error: null
  };
}
```

Exceptions

The other way of writing errors is throwing/catching exceptions. The idea of exceptions is in most programming languages. Exceptions are problems that happen when your program is running. You can write code to handle exceptions so your program does not suddenly stop or crash.

When handling exceptions, don't assume errors are all due to one type of error. In the example below, can you assume that the error in the `try/catch` is due to a missing user with that email?

```
try {
  const userJson = UserApi.findByEmail(email);
  const user = JSON.parse(userJson);
  return user;
} catch(err) {
  printError('Missing user with that email.');
}
```

How did we assume the error was due to a missing user? What if the problem was the JSON parsing? For handling exceptions, it's best to catch all known exceptions so when you have to see the error message, you'll know why the program failed.

```
try {
  const userJson = UserApi.findByEmail(email);
  const user = JSON.parse(userJson);
  return user;
} catch(Exception err) {
    if (err instanceof SyntaxError) {
      printError('Error parsing JSON.');
    } else if (err instanceof NotFoundException) {
      printError('Missing user with that email.');
    } else {
      printError('Unknown exception ${err.getMessage()}');
    }
}
```

Testing

When you give other people your program, you realize they may not input what you think.

If you wrote a function to accept two variables and add them. You expected the inputs to just be numbers, but what if a user passed in strings?

What would your function do?

Unit tests are a way of showing people what the expected outputs are given an input.

Unit tests are especially important when you decide to optimize your program to make it faster. In the process of optimizing your program, you could have introduced a bug. If you have many unit tests, these bugs are easier to catch to ensure the correctness of your program.

Design Patterns

Design patterns are ways of organizing your code. They aren't how to solve problems but rather how to organize your solution in a conventional manner. Algorithms are how to solve a problem and design patterns are how to structure your algorithm in a presentable and conventional way.

I won't go into detail here since this topic is a book in itself. Just be aware of the term and that design patterns are documented heavily with examples.

Be also aware that programmers can misuse design patterns and organize simple code into a complicated mess.

Writing Pull Requests

If you are working with a larger project, you'll most likely be using Git.

Git has the concept of a pull request where you submit your suggested changes to the project.

The programmers on the project will comment on your pull request and ask you to make changes. When they feel it is of enough quality and usefulness, they can merge your pull request into the project.

You would be submitting your pull request wherever the project is hosted, most likely Github or Gitlab.

When you are writing your pull request, include why you wrote this addition to the project, what it does and how to test it.

Conversely, sometimes you will find yourself on the other side where you are asked to review pull requests. As the reviewer, you are responsible for understanding what the pull request is for and testing it. Reviewing other people's code in pull requests is a great way to learn how to solve a specific issue.

Output files

Along with writing better code, consider the format of your output. Your data files will most likely outlive the programs you write. Output the data in a standard file format. Don't invent your own formats because if you give your data output file to someone else, they will not be able to easily parse the file to use in their programs.

Common data file formats to use are: csv, json, xml. You can also store data into a database.

If you want to share your program output to a non-programmer who knows Excel, you might want to consider writing the output as a CSV file.

If your output is records of text data and your collaborators are programmers, JSON could be better.

Using a database is useful when your data has sets of related data. One example could be a large list of authors and book details. With the database, you can let your collaborator query the database to find different patterns like "Which author wrote the most books in the 1980s".

Examples of Writing and Reading Data

CSV

```
import csv

with open('books.csv', 'wt') as outfile:
    writer = csv.writer(outfile, delimiter=',')
    writer.writerow(['1', 'a tale of two cities'])
    writer.writerow(['2', 'the three body problem'])

with open('books.csv') as infile:
    reader = csv.reader(infile, delimiter=",")
    for row in reader:
      print(row)
```

JSON

```
import json

data = {
    "books": [
        {"id": 1, "title": "a tale of two cities"},
        {"id": 2, "title": "the three body problem"},
    ]
}

with open("books.json", "w") as outfile:
    json.dump(data, outfile)

with open("books.json") as infile:
    data = json.load(infile)
    for book in data["books"]:
        print(book)
```

SQL Database

```
import sqlite3

conn = sqlite3.connect('mysqlite.db')
c = conn.cursor()

c.execute('''CREATE TABLE IF NOT EXISTS books
             (id real, title text)''')

c.execute('''INSERT INTO books
             VALUES(1, 'a tale of two cities'),
             VALUES(2, 'the three body problem');
             ''')

c.execute('''SELECT * FROM documents ''')
rows = c.fetchall()

for row in rows:
    print(row)

conn.commit()
conn.close()
```

Differences with Files in Windows vs Mac/Linux

If you are sharing text files with someone who uses Windows, you may notice strange characters at the end of each line.

Windows and Mac/Linux systems use a different character to mark the end of a line. You may have to run **dos2unix** or **unix2dos** to convert the file before usage.

Chapter 8

Getting Help

How to Ask

"a perfect formulation of a problem is already half its solution."

— David Hilbert

If you ask someone for help and just say "it does not work", that will not be very helpful for you or the other person you asked for help.

Think about how you want to ask the question. What was the input? What was the incorrect output? What should be the correct output? How did you try to solve the issue? Did you try different inputs?

There's a concept known as "rubber duck debugging" where if you spend time to explain your problem to someone else, you end up finding the solution yourself while you explaining the problem.

Figure 8.1: Reading other people's code. Art from http://abstrusegoose.com/432

Reproduce the Problem

It is also helpful if you are able to reproduce the exact issue to show someone. If you cannot reproduce the problem, others will find it difficult to know how to help.

Share your code through a tool like Visual Studio Codespaces so they can see the reproduced error.

Where to Get Help

Search engines are the first place to start asking for help. Figuring out what to type into the search box will take experience and practice to see what gives you the best results. You may have to reformulate your search query many times to get the pages you expect.

The search results will contain sources from: * StackOverflow.com: Good for the quick answers with validation from other peers. * The project documentation: Project documentation will vary depending on the project itself. One downside is that most documentation do not include comments from other programmers so it will be hard to determine if the section you are reading is related to your problem. * Blog articles: Also a varying source dependent on the writer. Also, beware if the solution is out of date. * Books: Books tend to be good if you really want to understand a topic or concept but less useful if you need an answer to a question. Use book sources if the stackoverflow answer makes no sense.

You can also ask in web communities like reddit.com or Discord chat.

Reporting a Problem

First, make sure the problem you encountered is a problem of the software you are using and not from your code referencing it improperly.

A problem in the code is also known as a bug. To make a bug report usable, isolate your code with just enough code to reproduce your problem.

The project will have a page you report bugs to. Reporting bugs allows the owner or another contributor to fix your problem. Why would they fix your problem for free? Probably because if you are experiencing this bug, someone else will be too.

Most projects will have a place to report bugs like:

- Github Issues
- JIRA

Is the Help Correct?

Be careful of just using Google. Don't accept the first link as the answer. Sometimes you get sources like w3schools.com which is an inferior source of help than Mozilla Developer Network. Stackoverflow and its StackExchange partner sites are also good sources.

Make sure the answer is updated as software changes over time. An answer for an Android programming question will be different from 2010 to 2016.

Read multiple answers. Don't assume the first answer is the most suited. There are different approaches to solving one problem.

You will copy and paste code from Stack Overflow. We all do it. Just take the time to understand each parameter and variable by reading the docs or commenting on the stackoverflow question.

Chapter 9

Debugging Code

A Method for Solving a Problem

Once you write a lot of code, you will run into unexpected
errors and bugs. Debugging is the process of finding the cause
of a problem given a visible symptom.

The most naive strategy is: 1. See an unexpected symptom 2.
Try changing something that you think might be causing the
error 3. Re-run the program 4. If it works, great! If it doesn't,
repeat from step 2 until it works.

Almost everyone debugs this way and it will work most of
the time especially if you have enough experience to have a
reasonable thought what is causing the issue.

By having a more systematic debugging process for solving a
problem, you make debugging a deliberate practice as opposed
to trying random variable changes in hopes it works.

For extensive help on debugging, take a look at David J Agans'
Debugging: The 9 Indispensable Rules for Finding Even the
Most Elusive Software and Hardware Problems

Below are some methods and tools to help you debug better.

The Error Message

Often the error message may not be directly related to your actual bug. This can make debugging a little more difficult to narrow down.

When you run this python program:

```
1 cat_is_fed = True
2
3 if (cat_is_fed):
4   print('yes'
5 else:
6   print('no')
```

We see this error message:

```
> python cat.py
  File "cat.py", line 5
    else:
      ^
SyntaxError: invalid syntax
```

If we read the error explicitly, it is misleading because there is nothing wrong with line 5 `else:` However, if we look at the previous line, there is a missing) which ends the `print` function.

Be mindful of these misleading messages and do not assume the bug is on the exact line reported by the error message.

Make Small Changes

If you are fixing a problem, make a small change. Ensure your program still works and then repeat. The larger the changes you make, the more you risk side-effect changes.

Ensure Each Function Works as Expected

When you know your program is not working as expected but you don't know where the issue is, you can start hypothesizing which function is unexpectedly giving you the wrong result. Start calling functions with different inputs to see if the function output matches your expectations.

Unit Testing

Having a suite of unit tests that you can run easily is important to ensure that when you "fix" a bug, it does not cause a regression in breaking other known working code.

Each programming language approaches unit testing differently.

Here's an example of a Python unit test which tests the string method `isupper()`

```python
import unittest

class TestStringMethods(unittest.TestCase):
    def test_isupper(self):
        self.assertTrue('FOO'.isupper())
        self.assertFalse('Foo'.isupper())
if __name__ == '__main__':
    unittest.main()
```

Sourced from docs.python.org/3/library/unittest.html

Imagine you wrote the `isupper()` function and you had to fix an issue inside the function. After you make your fix, you can run this unit test again to ensure that both test cases are still valid.

Use a Debugger

A debugger is a tool that lets you follow your program as it runs each line of code. At each line, you can see the contents of the memory. This lets you see if there's a variable set to a value you didn't expect.

Each programming language has a debugger. For Java, it tends to be built into the editor like InteliJ. For Python, the debugger is called pdb.

Print Statements or Logging

Adding logging statements is helpful to see if the variables and function outputs are what you expect.

You can use the standard print functions like `print` in Python or `console.log` in Node.

Alternatively, you use the language's logging libraries. Here's an example of using the built-in logging library in Python:

```python
import logging
logging.basicConfig()

logger = logging.getLogger(__name__)
logger.setLevel(logging.DEBUG)

def split_name(name=''):
    fname, lname = name.split(' ')
    return {'first_name': fname, 'last_name': lname}

name = 'John Galt'
logger.info('create_user with {0}'.format(name))
entry = split_name(name)
logger.info('split_name returned {0}'.format(entry))
```

Here is the program's output showing the logging messages:

```
> python test.py
INFO:__main__:create_user with John Galt
INFO:__main__:split_name returned
{'first_name': 'John', 'last_name': 'Galt'}
```

Using a logging library is helpful because you can configure the logging to output to different sources and to optionally turn them off. In the example above, we set it to output to the screen but we could have configured it to output to a separate file instead.

Explain the Problem

If you cannot explain the problem and why the problem is happening, then the problem is too complex for you. This is an opportunity for you to read and research more about the topic to get a better understanding of the problem.

Common Language Bugs

Data Types

Some languages don't require you to specify a data type for a variable like Python or Ruby. These languages just let you assign a variable like x = 1 or x = 'hi'

This does reduce the amount of thinking time when using variables but it comes at the price of possible bugs.

When you write functions:

```
def add(x, y):
    return x + y
```

What happens if you pass in a string and an integer?

In languages that don't require you to specify a type(these languages are known as dynamically typed), they handle these cases differently. Some will try to cast the string to an integer and add it, some will cast the integer to a string and perform a string concatenation. Be mindful of how your language handles these cases.

Equality

What does it mean for two values to be equal?

In terms of primitive values like integers, we can be assured that if `x = 1` and `y = 1` that `x == y`

What about `x = 1` and `y = '1'`(note the string), does `x == y`?

Many programming languages will automatically convert data types for you. This is known as implicit type coercion because you do not see the actual process of converting data types. Sometimes this has helpful behavior, sometimes it can be the source of bugs.

Javascript offers a type checked equality check (===) to avoid this implicit type coercion:

```
console.log(`true === 1: ${true === 1}`);
```

outputs

```
true === 1: false
```

when we start checking equality for objects and classes, the equality check can lead to unexpected results.

In Java, if you have two objects like `Car x = new Car("Tesla")` and `Car y = new Car("Tesla")`, `x == x` but `x == y` is false.

With `==` Java checks the memory address of the object for equality.

If you want to check equality against the actual values, you must use a builtin method: `x.equals(y)`.

Check how your language handles the `==` operator before you use it.

Chapter 10

Solving Your Problem

Before you even try to solve a problem with your own code, do a search to make sure someone else has not already solved your problem.

Don't Rewrite Code

Has someone already done exactly what you want?

Generally, over 80% of your coding problems have already been solved.

If you have time or want to develop your coding skills, it is a useful exercise to code the solution and compare it against other solutions online. Is your code easier to understand? Is it more efficient?

Do the Research

It is very rare you will be writing a solution by scratch. Programming is more like building with Legos. You use prebuilt pieces to build from. In traditional universities, you are taught programming from the ground up. It's a useful learning experience but it's not what you'll be doing in day to day programming tasks.

This means you need to learn to read and understand other people's code. What if you found a solution but it's in another language? That's ok, you can still read the code for a better understanding of the problem.

Open Source

Most of the programming pieces you will use are open source packages. Being an open source package can mean many things including free to use for anything or just free for non-commercial use. I'm not a lawyer so I can't advise on the particular details of open source licenses for your usage. Generally, there are a few popular ones: MIT, Apache, GPL. Each has their particular restrictions with the MIT license being one of the more less restrictive one.

Why are there so many possible solutions?

When you look up how to write a particular code, you'll have many solutions to choose from. Your job will be to determine which solution is most suitable for your needs.

Some useful tips on choices:

- If deciding which code library to use, pick the more popular one. For example, on Github, select the one with more stars.
- How out-dated is the solution? Try the articles with a more recent publication date.

- Can you understand the solution? Don't just copy and paste any code. If you can't understand it, you may need to debug it in the future.

Use the Right Language

Since you are a beginning programmer, you probably learned the basics of one language like Python, Ruby or Javascript.

A secret of successful programmers is the ability to pick and choose the tools that most easily and efficiently solve their problems.

This might mean learning a new programming language to accomplish a goal.

For example, consider the case when you want to create graphs for your science paper from a set of data. You can do it in Ruby or Javascript, but you could probably have an easier job using the ggplot2 package in R to create better designed graphs.

Conversely, if you were expected to make a web application, you wouldn't use R. Javascript and Ruby/Python would be more suitable options.

When do you decide you don't know enough?

When you are teaching yourself programming, you most likely are doing it by example. Find an example on the Internet, copy and paste it and change things around until it does what you want. This works well where you don't need a complete understanding of the example. It is also a really fast way of getting things done. This method will be problematic when you start seeing many bugs or performance issues. At this point, you will need to start understanding how the code works to be able to effectively change the code to work. At this point, you need to spend time to understand the deeper concepts of your project.

Have a Plan

Spend a little time planning out what you are going to write and the parts of the problem.

If someone asks you to write a program to convert a recipe from American units(oz) to metric units(grams), can you think of the possible parts of the problem?

Here's one decomposition of the problem into smaller units:

1. Parsing each line of the recipe
2. Extract the measurement number from the line
3. Convert the measurement from oz to grams
4. Print the output

Make Mistakes

Don't be afraid of making mistakes, make a lot of them early on and learn why the mistake happened. I find learning from mistakes as more informative than learning by the principles first for beginners to avoid being overwhelmed.

Chapter 11

Writing Efficient Code

This chapter will show some tips for writing efficient and faster code.

The first question you need to ask is if you actually need to make your code run faster. If you just need to run the code once a month and it takes 10 minutes, maybe the time investment isn't worth it.

Your first job as a programmer is to make your program do what you want correctly. After you have established the correctness of the program, actually write tests to test different possible inputs.

Once you are confident it actually works and you have tests to verify the correctness, you can begin to make your code more efficient and faster.

Premature optimization is the source of many failed projects so again, make sure it works as much as you can first.

Trade-offs of Optimized Code

A program needs CPU and memory to run. Usually, these are the trade-offs: a program can use more memory and less CPU or less memory and more CPU. You need to know what you want to optimize for.

Using Faster Code vs Writing It Yourself

In my experience, I find the most effective way to make your code faster is to use a library, data structure or algorithm that has been used for years. It is rare for programmers to come up with a new algorithm which is faster than the one that has already been used for years or decades.

Edge Cases

Edge cases are situations you do not initially anticipate. For example, if you are given an equation like $(2 / x) * 200 + 1$, you may naively write:

```
def math_fun(x):
    return ( 2 / x ) * 200 + 1
```

Some edge cases you want to test are the limits of the input parameter x. We can try running the function with x as negative numbers, zero and really large numbers.

We see that the function we wrote fails on some of these edge cases. How you handle the edge cases is up to you. The least you can do is return back a nicer error message explaining why the function failed.

```
def math_fun(x):
```

```
if x == 0:
    throw \You cannot use 0 as an input"
return ( 2 / x ) * 200 + 1
```

Packages/Libraries

Search for code packages/libraries for the right functions and data structures before trying to write your own.

For example, Python has a package called numpy which contains many math functions.

Common algorithms

The most common algorithms are already built into the languages. For example, if you need to sort an array of numbers or find the largest value in a number, it's most likely an easy one line solution like `[5,2,9,1].sort()` or `[5,2,9,1].max()`

Data structures

A data structure is the formatting of how data is stored, searched and fetched.

Each data structure has its pros and cons in terms of storage and speed.

Which data structure should you use? That depends on what you want to do with the data.

These are the most common and basic data structures that you want to know.

- Hash Map (or Hash Table or Dictionary)

A hash map is used for associating one key with a value.

Example:

```
>>> people = {}
>>> people['alice'] = 'apple'
>>> people['bob'] = 'durian'
>>> people['eve'] = 'orange'
```

You can then reference what value "bob" is associated with:

```
>>> people['bob']
```

- Set

Remember in Math classes when you had those Venn diagrams?

A set contains a non-duplicate list of items.

These are examples of using sets. It's a great way to store data when you want to see if an item is in different sets.

```
>>> items = ["apple", "durian", "orange", "apple"]
>>> items_set = set(items)
>>> items_set
set(['orange', 'apple', 'durian'])
>>> "durian" in items_set
True
>>> "jackfruit" in items_set
False
```

- Linked List

A linked list is a list where each item is connected to the one before and after it.

For a small set of items, using either set or list for finding an item in a group is sufficient but for larger groups, the set data structure will be faster.

Databases

Commonly, when you talk about the data structures mentioned above, they are referring to the data stored in memory.

When you have more information than it could be into your computer's memory, you need to start storing the information onto a computer's hard drive. The easiest way to store the information onto a computer's hard drive is just to write it to multiple files. Unfortunately, this becomes problematic once you want to get information out of these files.

Databases are data structures stored in files which allow you to get access to the information in an easier and more efficient manner.

Some popular databases include:

- Sqlite
- Mysql
- PostgreSQL

Cache

Sometimes you need to ask a database or a web api the same question over and over again.

A cache is a fixed size from a few megabytes for in-process caches like the node lru-cache package to a few GBs for cache servers like Memcache.

What is difficult about using a cache? Since caches have a fixed size, cache invalidation can be a problem. This means is the value in the cache the value it should be?

Here's an example of using an LRU Cache system:

```
getById(userId) {
  const cacheKey = `user-${userId}`;
```

```
if (!LRUCache.has(cacheKey)) {
  LRUCache.set(
      cacheKey,
      callToDatabaseOrWebService(userId)
  );
}

return LRUCache.get(cacheKey);
}
```

How fast is fast?

How can you think about knowing if your program is faster or not?

In Computer Science, there is a deep field for analyzing the performance of an algorithm. The most important measurement you need to know is O notation. Refer to the upcoming chapter "Important Computer Science Topics" for a review on this topic.

RAM vs Disk

Your computer has two types of memory storage: RAM and disk. RAM is 100,000x faster than the disk. Thus it is more optimal for your program to have all the working data it needs in RAM.

For example, if your program needs to work on a 100 MB file, it is ideal to load the file into memory instead of having to work off the disk.

Buffering

Sometimes, when you work with a really large file, say >1GB, you cannot load the file into memory because you will not have enough RAM space. You can use a concept known as "buffering" to load chunks of the file at a time, do some processing, writing that result to disk and repeating.

Chapter 12

Useful Computer Science Topics

These are a few topics you should be aware of, not necessarily be a master at, but definitely know they exist and you can learn more about them.

The Computer Science degree advantage is being aware of all of these topics. Knowing what you don't know is often troubling when you are presented with a problem. Computer science courses expose you to many types of problems, 80% of which you will never ever use since people tend to focus on a particular field, not jumping from one industry to another. Fact is that most programmers won't ever have to program an air traffic optimization problem, but the Computer Science courses will still teach these topics to you. Knowing this won't necessarily make you a better web programmer. This is why it's important to realize what your goals are to maximize what you learn can be applied to your job.

It also doesn't hurt to know a little about everything. The 4 year Computer Science degree(and furthermore if you get a masters or PhD) teaches you a lot about everything. Just spending a few minutes reading how problems exist can go a long way. In the future you can recognize the problem you are faced with can be solved with some particular mechanism, review it and implement it.

Big O Notation

Big O Notation is a formalized way of determining how your program behaves in terms of how much time it takes and how much memory it needs. In university, you would be asked to mathematically compute the O notation of a certain program.

In the real world, you just need to know how to do a rough estimation of your program in O Notation for the average case and worst case of inputs.

To summarize and not go too into depth, O-notation lets you know roughly the scale of how long an algorithm will take.

- $O(1)$ is constant, the best
- $O(\log n)$ is logarithmic - binary search
- $O(n)$ is linear - naive solution to finding an array
- $O(n \log n)$ is log linear - merge sort
- $O(n^2)$ is quadratic - naive bubble sort

If the number of input is very small(like less than 50 entries), any algorithm is fine.

But as you add more inputs into the algorithm, you want to choose an algorithm that is constant or linear, not polynomial and definitely not exponential.

Algorithms

Algorithms are the foundation of Computer Science. An algorithm is a set of instructions that describe how to accomplish a task.

They have many useful applications including Google's infamous search ranking algorithm, PageRank.

Fortunately as an aspiring programmer, you generally do not need to invent new algorithms in your day to day workflow.

The majority of the popular algorithms are already written in your programming language's standard libraries.

For example, to sort an array in Ruby:

```
[80, 30, 2222, 1].sort
```

This uses the `Quicksort` algorithm without you even needing to know about what `quicksort` is.

Khan Academy has a useful introduction to algorithms https://www.khanacademy.org/computing/computer-science/algorithms

While you may not use algorithms day to day, many companies will ask you to implement or apply one of the popular algorithms during interviews.

Compilers

Fundamentally, all the code you write is just a more efficient way of expressing your thoughts to the computer.

A computer processes a very simple and limited set of machine assembly commands like:

```
mov 1 $1
add $1 $2
mov $3 $1
```

The `if` statements, the `for` loops and functions you write all get compiled into these assembly commands for the computer.

Compilers will give you a deeper understanding of how programming languages work but it's unlikely you will need to write a compiler. The deeper understanding will help you debug programming problems easier.

For an introduction to programming in assembly, refer to Programming from the Ground Up: An Introduction to Programming using Linux Assembly Language

For the time investment involved, I would not recommend learning much about compilers unless you have a desire to learn how they work.

Operating Systems

You can think of Mac OSX/Unix and Linux as having the same underlying system. The basic commands like `ls`, `cd`, `grep` are all shared among these operating systems.

In principle, there are quite a number of differences. The only one you really need to know for now is which software management system each operating system uses.

Linux is mostly split between Debian-based and Red Hat-based. The Debian-based operating systems include the popular Ubuntu. These use `apt-get` while the Red Hat-based systems(Fedora, CentOS) uses `yum` for managing packages.

On a Mac, you can choose to use `brew`.

How a program in Unix works

When you run a program, Unix assigns it a PID (Process identifier).

You can use this PID to check the progress on it.

Most input and output operations in Unix environments can be abstracted to reading from a file or writing to a file where the `file` can be the screen or the keyboard.

When a program is terminated, either expected or unexpectedly, the program is given an exit code. If the exit code is 0, it means it was successful doing its job.

Programming Paradigms

Just like writing has different particular paradigms, writing code also has particular paradigms. A paradigm is a way of structuring and organizing code. When you write code, you will end using a variety of these different paradigms depending on the situation. You will commonly see different paradigms in one project.

These programming paradigms are independent of the actual language you use. You can write code in Javascript using imperative, object-oriented or functional paradigms.

Imperative Programming

This is the typical style used to teach people how to write code.

You write how the program should operate line by line.

The distinguishing trait of imperative programming is controlling the program's state.

A simple example of imperative programming is collecting the even numbers.

```
numbers = range(0, 10)
even_numbers = []
for num in numbers:
  if num % 2 == 0:
    even_numbers.append(num)
print(even_numbers)
```

The even_numbers variable is changed throughout the for loop.

Functional Programming

Functional paradigms are characterized by writing your code as pure functions that you can call upon. Pure functions are side-effect free meaning you do not alter any state. You generate new output from the existing input. This means that calling the same function again and again will output the same result.

For example, if you have a math function:

```
f(x) = (x + 1)^ 2
```

You know a few certain things: the parameter x will not change after you call this function. You can call this method twenty times and x will remain the same. If x were to change, this would be called a side-effect of the function.

Likewise, in the programming world, adopting these principles will really help you reduce the number of bugs. The more times you change a variable, the more likely a bug will occur.

This example below is the functional equivalent of collecting the even numbers. The variable even_numbers never changes and is only set once.

```
numbers = range(0, 10)
even_numbers = filter(lambda num: num % 2 == 0, numbers)
print(even_numbers)
```

Object-Oriented Programming

Object-Oriented Programming(OOP) can be considered a subset of imperative programming. You organize your code based on "classes" which represent a particular state.

For example, if your program is computing the daily fitness of a cat, you could create a class named Cat and keep track of its health attributes.

Inheritance and encapsulation are the key principles of OOP.

```
class Cat:
  def __init__(self):
    self.__times_fed = 0
```

```
  def feed(self):
    self.__times_fed += 1
    return self.__times_fed

  def is_hungry(self):
    return self.__times_fed == 0

mycat = Cat()
cat_fed = 'no' if mycat.is_hungry() else 'yes'
print('did i feed the cat? ' + cat_fed)
```

In the example below, the variable `__times_fed` is considered a private variable that is meant to be only altered by code inside the `Cat` class. Hiding this private variable from the public is known as encapsulation.

Inheritance lets you define a subclass to reuse the code from the base class.

This statement will create a new class and keep all the code from the `Cat` class: `class PersianCat(Cat):`

Graphs

Graphs and Graph Theory are very important topics in Computer Science. Do not confuse them with bar graphs, line graphs used in Excel spreadsheets. A graph in Computer Science refers to a representation of "vertices" connected by "edges".

Some use cases for graphs include representing airline travel routes or a company organization structure of which employee works with which group.

Databases

A database is an organized system for storing and accessing data. A database consists of many tables which consists of many rows.

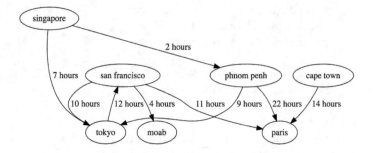

Figure 12.1: A Graph representing travel times, the vertices are the cities and the edges are the travel times

SQL

SQL (Standard Query Language) is used to write commands for asking a database for a set of results. The most common SQL databases are sqlite, MySQL and PostgreSQL. All of these allow you to use a similar set of SQL commands.

If you want to pursue a data science or data engineering career, learning SQL well is a must.

Indexing

A fundamental concept in databases is indexing. Indexing a column in a table makes a read query faster. Why not just index all the columns in a database? The downsides are that it will take more memory and it can make the database write operations slower.

Primary Key

In a database table, you will have one column which is automatically indexed. It is an important decision to decide what you want as your primary key as it will impact the performance of fetching and writing records to the database.

ORM

Object relational modeling(ORM) libraries translate common tasks like saving, finding records to SQL for you.

Here's an example of code writing to the database with Ruby on Rails' ActiveRecord ORM:

```
class Client < ApplicationRecord
  has_one :address
  has_many :orders
  has_and_belongs_to_many :roles
end

client = Client.new(name: "Jerry")
client.save
```

By calling .save, ActiveRecord will translate this to the SQL statement:

```
INSERT INTO clients(name) VALUES('Jerry');
```

Writing SQL statements can lead to many bugs including security issues. An ORM helps reduce this effort for the programmer.

Some of the other common ORMs are SQLAlchemy for Python, Sequelize for Nodejs.

Networking

A network is the group mechanism that connects devices together: computers, mobile phones and smart devices like the Google Home. The network allows these devices to communicate with each other. Networking is an extensive topic. You can get a dedicated career in managing networks.

The important topics that you will encounter as a programmer are:

- Internet Protocol, in particular what IP Addresses are.
- Domain Name System(DNS) and how it maps a domain to an IP address.
- HTTP and its secure counterpart HTTPS.

Chapter 13

Sharing Code

Now the next step, writing code that works more than once and on more than one computer. That's right: just because it works on your computer doesn't mean that it will instantly work on another computer.

How can I give my project to someone else to use?

Hosting your Project Online

The first step is just to put the project source code on Github.

Packaging your Project

Realize your computer is not the same as your friend's computer. Even if you both use Macbook Airs with Mountain Lion 10.7, there will be subtle differences that can cause problems.

Distribute your Project

Each language has its own central repository. You definitely want to publish your project here to get the most usage.

- R - https://cran.r-project.org
- Python -https://pypi.python.org/pypi
- Nodejs -https://npmjs.org
- Ruby - https://rubygems.org
- Java - https://search.maven.org

This lets another programmer type in something like `npm install lodash` to install the project.

Don't know how? Search `"packaging a [LANGUAGE] app"`

Talk about it

"If a tree falls in a forest and no one's around, does anyone hear it?"

Of course not, it doesn't matter if you wrote something great if no one's going to use your project. Write a blog post, put it on Github, Reddit and Twitter.

Chapter 14

Programming as a Career

Interviewing for a job is difficult. You and the company have to prove to each other you are the right fit for the job in about 5 hours.

It's especially difficult if you have little experience and no college degree. The interview process will favor the college graduate and education as most software engineers have these degrees. Self-taught programmers will be at a disadvantage when interviewing.

The Interview Structure

Typically, an interview consists of:

- A 15 minute call with a recruiter
- A one hour technical screening on phone or via coderpad.io
- A three hour on-site interview

The three hour on site interview consists of:

- System Design
- Behavioral
- Coding Challenge

For the system design question, you will be asked to design a system, preferably drawing a diagram to describe the design. Sample design questions can be "design a mobile login system" or "design a search engine for a shopping business".

For the behavioral section, this is more focused on how you work with others including product managers and designers. A typical behavioral question might "Tell us about a time when you disagreed with a co-worker and how you dealt with it".

Coding Challenges

The coding questions tend to be toy problems including:

- write a sudoku validator
- construct a binary tree from an in-order array.

You will unlikely ever write a sudoku validator in your programming career.

So why do companies have you do this?

One: it's a measure of how much you are willing to prepare.

Two: it's a standard question they can ask many people and judge.

So unfortunately, you will have to play the game and learn how to solve toy programming problems for interviews.

The coding challenges typically come from LeetCode.com. For practice, focus on the easy and medium problems.

Writing a Resume

The resume is typically a 1 page fact sheet about yourself.

Use it to highlight your skill-set and do not downplay yourself. You are responsible for all you list on your resume so be prepared to be asked about every item. If you list `Jenkins CI/CD` as a skill, be prepared to explain how you used the tool.

Your resume can be difficult to fill up if you have absolutely no prior programming jobs.

Some ways you can work around this:

- Can you get an internship for experience?
- Do you have a website with a portfolio?
- Can you demonstrate a self-created project?
- List your projects on Github.

A typical resume will have:

- Name
- Contact: phone, email and any web links(blog, github)
- One line summary: What type of role you are looking for.
- Work Experience: Company, work duration, accomplishments
- Projects
- Education
- List of Skills

How do you get an Interview

Do you know anyone in a company?

The most effective way to get a job is to have an internal employee refer you and be your champion inside the company. You will still need to be qualified to get through the interview process but having someone vouch for you is invaluable. If you don't know any employees, find these where the company's employees participate in. Does the company host local meetups or events?

Having the company recruiter reach out is another good option to get you started in the interview process.

Applying for the job on the company website is a last resort as it is very easy to get lost or overlooked in the resume sifting process.

Interview Preparation

Learn about what the company does. Visit the company's career site, visit their glassdoor.com profile and check out their engineering blog.

If they have a product, create an account and use it.

You can ask the recruiter or manager about the process and type of questions you can expect.

Does the interview consist of direct coding questions? Pair programming? Diagramming a system? Or a more traditional data structures and algorithms question?

Interview Tips

Not knowing the solution is not always an immediate rejection. If you know how to find the solution by using an Internet source, you could ask the interviewer if you look up something.

Ask questions for clarification. Sometimes the interview question isn't specified and has unstated assumptions.

Learn to explain what you are doing. Don't be quiet during the coding sessions. Your process is more important than the raw solution.

When given a coding question, you will be judged on correctness, efficiency and style and on your communication skills in describing your solution.

Get to the most simple solution that works first, then optimize. You can ask to solve a simpler version of the problem if needed.

Talk about the code as you are writing. This also builds rapport with the interviewers in getting them to understand how you think.

Have an opinion or rationale for things. Even if interviewers don't agree, it lets them know that you take the time to think about what you do as opposed to just accepting things blindly.

The Offer

If you passed the interview, you'll get an offer letter. Congrats!

The offer letter will specify the details of your job title, level and compensation.

The compensation consists of:

- Base salary: This is important because raises and future compensation will be based as a percentage on this number.
- Bonuses: This can be a hit or miss and comes with restrictions such as having to work for the company for a set time before actually getting anything. Sometimes the bonuses could be worth more than your salary.
- Benefits: Does your company offer insurance? perks? remote work policies?

Depending on your situation, you could be in a position to negotiate different parts of your offer. This is especially true if you have many offer letters from different companies. Ask the company of their job level chart and where you would be positioned. levels.fyi is a good public resource for finding a company's compensation scale. It never hurts to negotiate but be prepared with reasons to say why you are worth what you are asking for. Having multiple higher offers from different companies is a great way to negotiate.

Chapter 15

The Job Hunt

Ultimately the immediate team you would be working with should be the most important deciding factor for selecting a job.

The company can have the best or worst mission but your immediate team will be what you will be involved in day to day.

These people can improve your technical and people skills or make your life stressful.

Research and talk to the team before joining the company.

Interview at as many companies as you can. The interview process is a draining experience but a few months is worth investing in for what could be a few years in a job. I recommend getting a few practice interviews by applying to companies that are not your top choices. Don't accept the first offer you get unless it really is exceeding your expectations.

Remote Work

In today's world, you are able to find a job where you can work remotely from a different city than the main headquarters.

At the small company level, being able to work in the same office has big benefits. You can get an understanding when products change and why they change. You can have code reviews/discussions which can go quicker in person than over chat.

As a beginning programmer, try to avoid companies where you would be the only remote person.

At medium and larger companies, there is more of a support structure around remote work. There are more people to help review your code. More people to chat with.

Once you become more skilled, remote work benefits start to surface more. You are able to focus alone time on tasks.

With all that said, your life situation will also dictate if remote work is a big criteria for selecting a job.

Small-sized Companies

At small companies, you will be able to make a large impact on the company's future.

You'll get to decide which technologies to use since you are likely the only programmer or one of three.

Feedback on your code quality is hard to receive especially if your company's project is barely used. The other programmers would likely be busy as well.

Most of your code will be thrown away. A startup's problem mostly deals with finding the right product to develop rather than a technical challenge.

With a very small chance, a startup can grow really fast and you are a part of a team that has to scale it very quickly. This can greatly speed up your skills as a software engineer through trial and error.

At a smaller company, expect a lower salary with questionable equity.

Any company smaller than 20 developers would be a small company.

Medium-sized Companies

The medium-sized company is more likely to be established and your code will actually be used by people. This is an important factor in getting feedback for your work. This means knowing if your code actually works under various conditions beyond a basic set of testing.

I think medium-sized companies are the best environment for a beginning programmer to learn the most in a short amount of time. You will get to work on a mix of old projects and new projects.

Medium sized companies range from 20 to 100 developers.

Large-sized Companies

Working for a large company means you will have constraints. A lot of them.

Want to use the standard Java web framework like Java Spring Boot? Maybe or maybe not. Large companies usually set a standard set of technologies you are allowed and not allowed to use. This is for good reasons as other teams will have to help maintain your project.

You will be a cog in a very large wheel and the cog can be easily replaced. Sometimes the product you spent 8 months working on will never launch.

The interviews will be more difficult. They tend to have the Computer Science based interview questions such as those found on leetcode.com.

The benefits? You'll get access to a lot of resources for learning. You can ask many smart individuals for advice. Your code will

be reviewed. You will get to focus on spending time to write
better code. There will be plenty of tech talks to learn new
topics.

Chapter 16

Working on Teams

Programming isn't just about working with yourself. You will end up working on a team or giving your code to someone else to run.

Management

There will be good managers, bad managers, micro-managers and hands-off managers.

Getting prompt and useful feedback from your manager and your peers is a great way to improve yourself.

Most people who get elevated to management never received proper training so don't be surprised if your manager does not perform the typical manager duties. They could be learning as well. Don't feel intimidated to ask for feedback on your work and performance.

The Product Requirements Document

Sometimes there will be a specification given for your program you are tasked to write. Often this document will not be able to include all the possible scenarios. Think of edge cases and ask your colleagues about them, even as you encounter them. The sooner you ask questions, the better it is for everyone involved in resolving it. In a better scenario, you will be involved in the process of writing a requirements document early on.

Communication Failure

Communication is what fails when you start working in larger groups, not necessarily the code itself.

One case is when a team using your software thought it would support a certain input but you were never told this input had to work.

Deciding the integration method and format first is a one way to solve this.

For example, The designer gives you the design file and you are asked to implement a signup form. If there is no specification, the first step is talk to the backend engineer.

How will the data from the signup form get sent to the server? What format is the server expecting? How will errors get returned from the server?

What you should not do is to start implementing the designs. There could be a lot of assumptions you are making which could cause you to make a time consuming or unnecessary solution.

Read Peopleware to learn more about how to work with people on a software project.

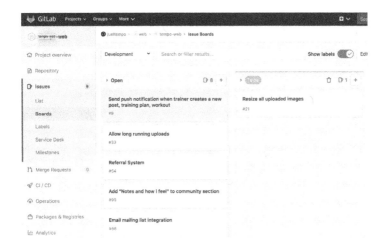

Figure 16.1: Gitlab Project Management

Project Tracking

In a team, you will be working with a project tracking tool like JIRA. These web-based software allows your team to break a project into sub-projects and tasks. The manager will assign tasks to individuals such as yourself.

When you are asked to create a ticket for something you will be doing, you need to be able to describe what the task is and an estimated plan of it succinctly. This will help start conversations if others have different opinions of what the task should be or suggestions on how it can be solved.

When you are reporting a bug, be as descriptive as possible. Saying "It returns an error" is not sufficient. You need to provide the exact error message(a screenshot or video is helpful), log messages related to the error, what should be the expected behavior and why the issue should be resolved.

Chapter 17

Final Words

"Wisdom is not a product of schooling but of the lifelong attempt to acquire it."

— Albert Einstein

As a parting thought, learning to write useful code will be a long and laborious process. Learn to make the journey enjoyable to ensure you keep learning. Part of being a good programmer is your ability to want to learn different techniques, systems and concepts.

Have fun learning!